Community Helpers During COVID-19

Volunteers
During COVID-19

Robin Johnson

CRABTREE
PUBLISHING COMPANY
WWW.CRABTREEBOOKS.COM

CRABTREE
PUBLISHING COMPANY
WWW.CRABTREEBOOKS.COM

Author: Robin Johnson
Series research and development:
  Janine Deschenes
Editorial director: Kathy Middleton
Editor: Janine Deschenes
Proofreader: Melissa Boyce
Graphic design: Katherine Berti
Image research: Robin Johnson
Print coordinator: Katherine Berti

Images:
Getty Images
    Anadolu Agency: p. 18 (top)
    Europa Press News: p. 11
    Ezequiel Becerra: p. 10 (bottom)
    Gerard Julien: p. 15
    Scott Olson: p. 12
Shutterstock
    Alison Ng: p. 3 (sign), 21 (top right)
    Bill Morson: p. 9 (bottom)
    Chadolfski: p. 4 (bottom)
    Fikri Yusof: p. 14 (bottom)
    Helissa Grundemann: p. 20 (bottom)
    Iron97: p. 16
    Manoej Paateel: p. 23 (top right)
    Oluwafemi Dawodu: p. 6 (top)
    Peryn22: p. 13 (top)
    Ron Adar: p. 6 (bottom)
    Sara Carpenter: p. 8 (bottom)
    Songdech Kothmongkol: p. 7 (top)
    Sumit Saraswat: p. 7 (bottom)
    TRKCHON STUDIO: p. 9 (top)
    Yaw Niel: p. 4 (top)
All other images by Shutterstock

Library and Archives Canada Cataloguing in Publication

Title: Volunteers during COVID-19 / Robin Johnson.
Names: Johnson, Robin (Robin R.), author.
Description: Series statement: Community helpers during COVID-19 |
    Includes index.
Identifiers: Canadiana (print) 20200390805 |
    Canadiana (ebook) 20200390813 |
    ISBN 9781427128348 (hardcover) |
    ISBN 9781427128386 (softcover) |
    ISBN 9781427128423 (HTML)
Subjects: LCSH: COVID-19 (Disease)–Juvenile literature. | LCSH: Volunteers–
    Juvenile literature. | LCSH: Epidemics–Social aspects–Juvenile literature. |
    LCSH: Community life–Juvenile literature.
Classification: LCC RA644.C67 J644 2021 | DDC j614.5/92414–dc23

Library of Congress Cataloging-in-Publication Data

Available at the Library of Congress

Crabtree Publishing Company
www.crabtreebooks.com   1-800-387-7650

Printed in the U.S.A./012021/CG20201112

**Published
in Canada**
Crabtree Publishing
616 Welland Ave.
St. Catharines, Ontario
L2M 5V6

**Published in the
United States**
Crabtree Publishing
347 Fifth Ave.
Suite 1402-145
New York, NY 10016

**Published in the
United Kingdom**
Crabtree Publishing
Maritime House
Basin Road North, Hove
BN41 1WR

**Published
in Australia**
Crabtree Publishing
Unit 3 – 5 Currumbin Court
Capalaba
QLD 4157

Contents

A Spreading Sickness

A **disease** called COVID-19 began to make people sick in 2019. The disease spread quickly from person to person. Soon people all around the world were sick. It became a **pandemic**.

This helper is telling people to stay home during the pandemic.

This worker is cleaning people's hands to help stop COVID-19 from spreading.

The leaders of countries told people how to stay safe. They said people should wash their hands often and try to stay home. Outside their homes, people should wear masks on their faces. They should keep a safe distance away from others.

In some countries, leaders decided there should be a **lockdown** for a period of time. Places such as stores were closed. People had to stay home as much as they could.

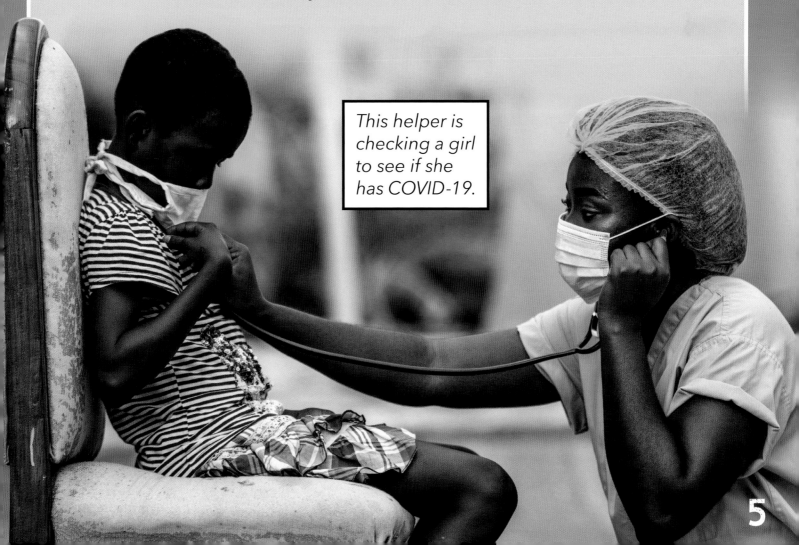

This helper is checking a girl to see if she has COVID-19.

Community Helpers

People in every community have worked together during the pandemic. A community is a group of people who live, work, and play in the same area. People make sure everyone can stay safe and meet their needs.

These helpers are giving out boxes of food.

These helpers are handing out free face masks in their community.

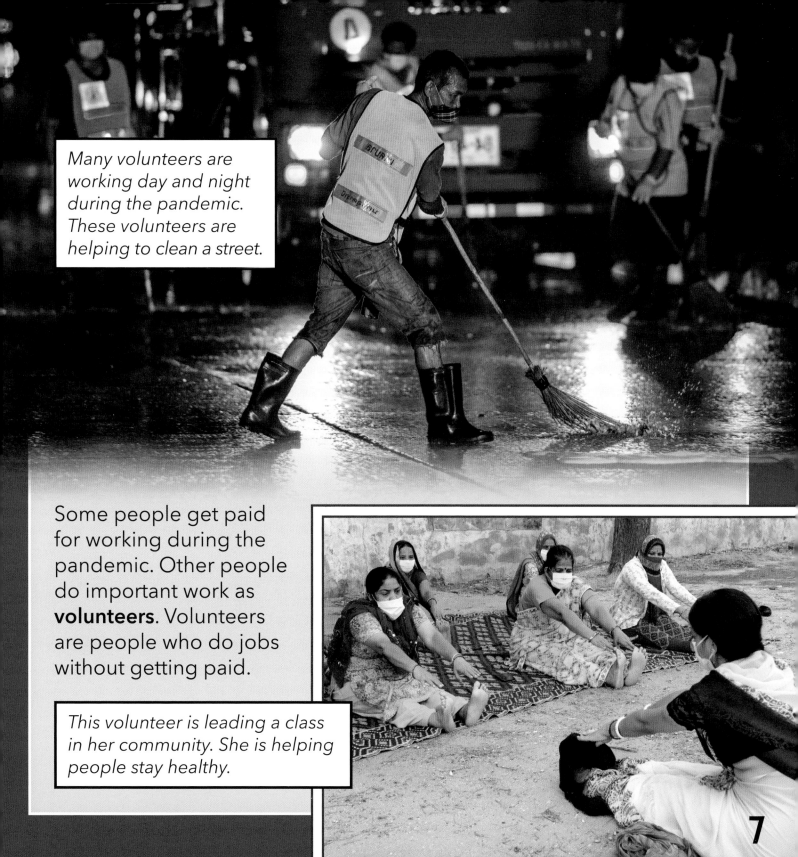

Many volunteers are working day and night during the pandemic. These volunteers are helping to clean a street.

Some people get paid for working during the pandemic. Other people do important work as **volunteers**. Volunteers are people who do jobs without getting paid.

This volunteer is leading a class in her community. She is helping people stay healthy.

Food for All

People have a **basic need** for food and clean water. Some people do not have enough money to buy food during the pandemic. Volunteers help make and give food to people who need it.

Many people **donate** food to give to those who need it.

These helpers set up a food **pantry** in their community. People can drive up and get the food they need.

These helpers are giving food and water to people.

Some volunteers work at food banks in their communities. Food banks are places where large amounts of donated food are kept. Other volunteers hand out free food in churches, gyms, or other buildings. Others load food right into people's cars!

This volunteer is picking vegetables for a food bank.

Safe Shelter

People have a basic need for **shelter**. They need somewhere safe, warm, and dry to live. Having shelter is very important during the pandemic. People who are sick need places to rest and get better.

Volunteers gather supplies for shelters. They make sure people have beds, blankets, and other things they need.

Volunteers helped change this gym into a place for people to stay.

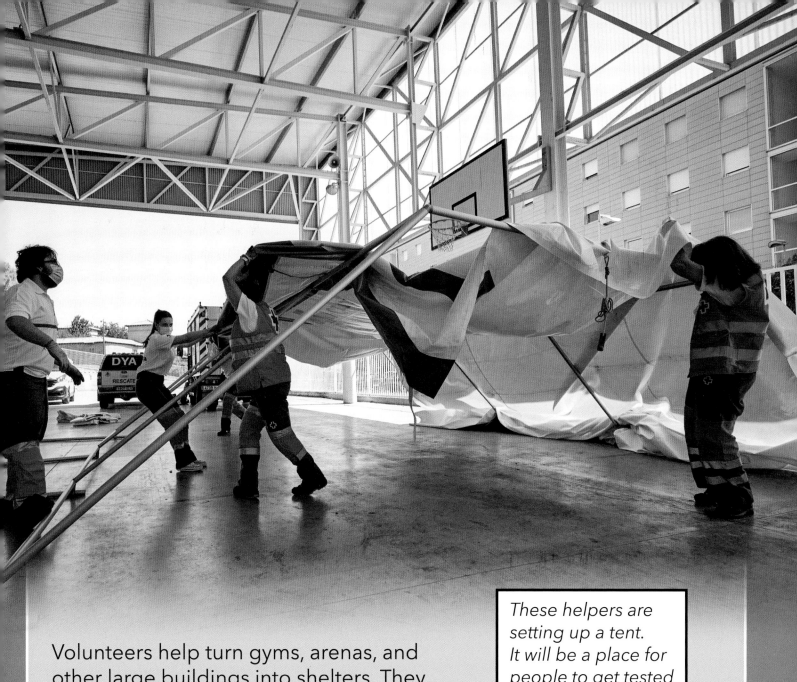

Volunteers help turn gyms, arenas, and other large buildings into shelters. They also build tents in communities. Some of the tents are used for people to live in for a while. Others are used for testing or looking after people with COVID-19.

These helpers are setting up a tent. It will be a place for people to get tested for COVID-19.

Health Care

People need to be cared for when they are sick. Many people are getting sick with COVID-19 all at once. Volunteers help doctors and nurses take care of them. They work in busy hospitals and many other places.

These volunteers collect blood for hospitals. They are working in a museum because hospitals are too crowded.

This volunteer is checking on a woman at home. He wants to make sure she is okay.

Some volunteers test people to see if they have COVID-19. Others give people information about the disease. Volunteers work hard to warn people and stop the disease from spreading.

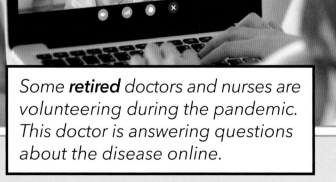

Some **retired** doctors and nurses are volunteering during the pandemic. This doctor is answering questions about the disease online.

Making a Difference

People need **equipment** to stay safe during the pandemic. Volunteers are helping to make the equipment. Some helpers make masks so people can cover their mouths and noses. Some helpers make gloves and suits for health care workers.

This volunteer is making face masks for people in his community.

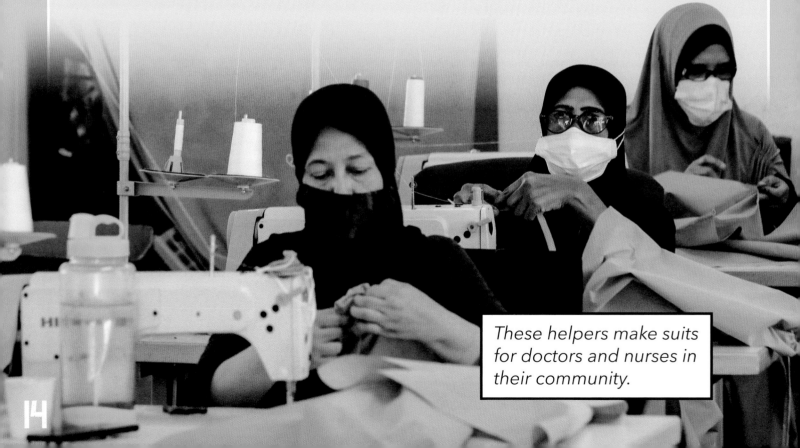

These helpers make suits for doctors and nurses in their community.

Some people with COVID-19 have trouble breathing. They need machines in hospitals to help them get enough air. Volunteers are working together to **design** and make these important machines.

These volunteers are designing a new machine to help people breathe.

Special Delivery

Volunteers are helping people get the supplies they need during the pandemic. Some helpers collect boxes of masks, gloves, and other supplies. They load the boxes onto trucks. Then they deliver them to hospitals and other places.

These volunteers are loading equipment onto a truck. They will deliver the equipment to hospitals.

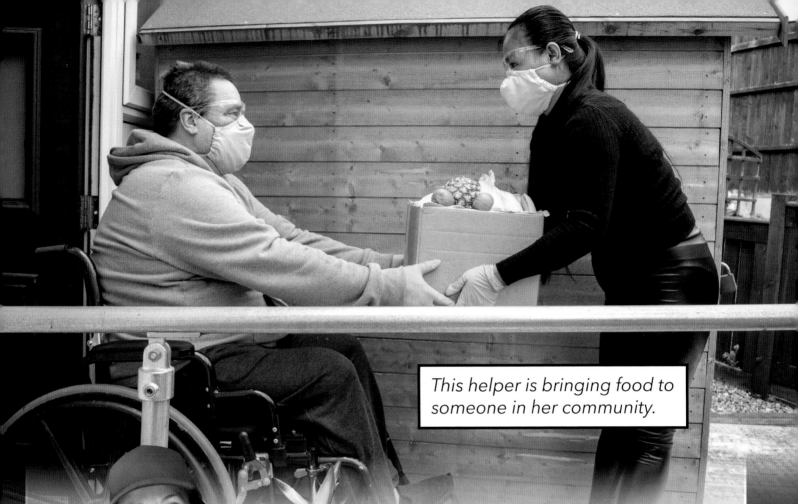

This helper is bringing food to someone in her community.

Some volunteers go shopping for people who cannot go to stores. They pick up food, medicine, and other supplies. Then they deliver everything right to people's homes.

Some volunteers deliver flowers to cheer people up.

This volunteer is looking after dogs at an animal shelter.

Pet Care

Pets have basic needs too! They need food to eat and water to drink. They need safe shelter and medicine. Volunteers make sure cats, dogs, and other pets get the care they need.

This helper is caring for a kitten until she can find a good home for it.

Some people cannot look after their pets during the pandemic. Volunteers care for these pets at places called animal shelters. Helpers also take pets home to look after them for a while.

Helpers care for pets during the pandemic. And pets make helpers happy!

Spreading Joy

COVID-19 spread quickly around the world. But people spread **joy** just as fast! Volunteers are finding many ways to make people feel happy during the pandemic.

THANK YOU

HEALTH CARE WORKERS

Libraries were closed during lockdowns. Helpers left books outside so people could keep reading.

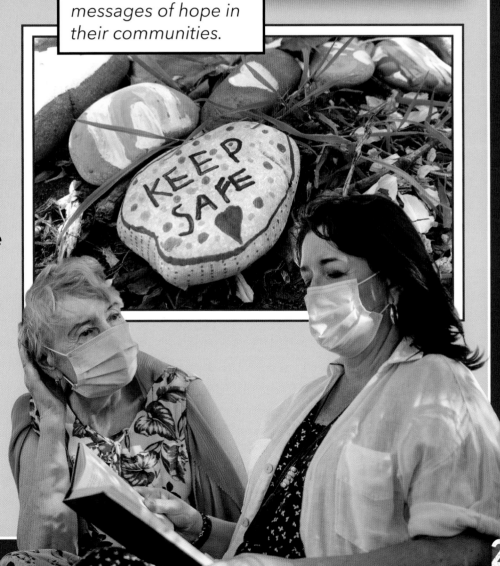

Children are spreading messages of hope in their communities.

Some helpers share books or puzzles. Others sing songs or make music to cheer people up. Children draw hearts and rainbows on windows and sidewalks. There are messages of **hope** and love in every community.

This volunteer is reading a book to a woman. The story brings her joy.

Glossary

basic need Something that people cannot live without

design To make a plan for how something is made or built

disease A sickness that prevents a person's body from working as it should

donate To give something to someone who needs it

equipment Supplies or tools needed for a special purpose

hope A feeling that something good will happen

joy A feeling of great happiness

lockdown A rule for people to stay where they are

pandemic A disease spreading over the whole world or a very wide area, such as many countries

pantry A small room or place where food is kept

retired Not working anymore

shelter A structure that covers or protects people

volunteer A person who does work without getting paid

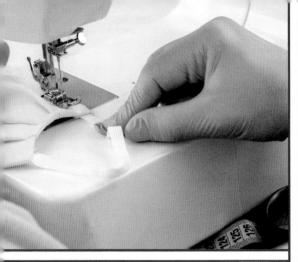

Index

About the Author

Robin Johnson is a freelance author and editor who has written more than 100 published children's books. She was fortunate to work from home during the pandemic and is grateful to all the helpers who kept her community running and her family safe.

Notes to Parents and Educators

Volunteers During COVID-19 celebrates the brave volunteers who are helping members of their communities stay safe, feel hopeful, and meet their basic needs for food, water, health care, and shelter. Below are suggestions to help children make connections and develop their reading and social studies skills.

Before reading

Show children the cover of the book. Ask children:

- What is a volunteer?

- Can a child be a volunteer? Why or why not?

- What is the girl on the cover doing? How is she helping others in her community?

During reading

After reading pages 6 and 7, review each image and turn to the glossary definition of volunteer. Ask children:

- What have you learned about volunteers? What kind of work do they do?

- Why are volunteers important parts of their communities?

After reading

Collaborate to make a list of the different ways volunteers are helping their communities during COVID-19.

Review pages 20 and 21. Invite children to work together to create a plan to spread joy, hope, and love in their community.